MYSTERY!

MYSTERY!

Visitors from Space

Katie Dicker

W

FRANKLIN WATTS
LONDON · SYDNEY

An Appleseed Editions book

First published in 2015 by Franklin Watts
338 Euston Road, London NW1 3BH

Created by Appleseed Editions Ltd,
Well House, Friars Hill, Guestling,
East Sussex TN35 4ET

Designed by Hel James
Edited by Mary-Jane Wilkins

Designed by Hel James
Edited by Mary-Jane Wilkins

Cataloging-in-Publication Data is available from the British Library

ISBN 978-1-4451-4180-0
Dewey Classification 001.9'42

Photo acknowledgements
title page Watchtheworld; page 3 Giordano Aita; 4-5 Esteban De Armas/
all Shutterstock; 8 Rodney_X/Thinkstock; 9 andrea crisante; 10-11
Zsolt Biczo; 11 Photobank gallery; 13 Neftali; 14 Albert Ziganshin; 15
Snaprender/all Shutterstock; 16 Nikita Sobolkov/Thinkstock; 18 MWaits;
19 photoBeard; 20 fstockfoto/
all Shutterstock; 21 Ingram Publishing/Thinkstock; 22-23 Photobank
gallery; 24 Watchtheworld/both Shutterstock
Cover diversepixel/Shutterstock

Artwork Q2A Media Art Bank

Printed in China

Franklin Watts is a division of Hachette Children's Books,
an Hachette UK company
www.hachette.co.uk

Contents

Space creatures

People have searched the skies for hundreds of years. Some have seen flashing lights and other strange objects. Could they have **witnessed** life from another planet?

Different planets

The **Universe** is full of thousands of millions of stars, just like our Sun. Many of these stars probably have planets circling them. There could be lots of planets like Earth out there, full of life. Perhaps we can get in touch with these space creatures?

Flying objects

Many people think that aliens
have visited Earth. They
claim to have seen alien
spacecraft, met aliens
or to have been inside
an alien spacecraft.
For hundreds of years,
people have seen objects
and lights in the sky.
We call them UFOs –
unidentified flying objects.

Some people say
they have met aliens
from outer space.

Flying objects

People have spotted all sorts of alien spacecraft. There have been reports of whirling wheels of fire, giant discs and tubes flying through the sky. Perhaps one day you'll see one of these strange objects!

Different theories

Thousands of years ago, people thought that mysterious lights and shapes in the sky were dragons or angels. Sometimes they thought the lights were from heaven or hell. Today, many people think these sightings could have been aliens.

All shapes and sizes

In the 1880s, people in Europe and the USA started seeing UFOs shaped like cigars. Some people said these spacecraft were full of aliens speaking a strange language. Today, sightings of flying saucers are more common. These disc-shaped spacecraft are usually silver, with a dome on the top full of windows.

In 1897, James Hooton saw a strange spaceship on the ground in Homan, Arkansas. This is a drawing of what he saw.

Some people report seeing disc-shaped spaceships.

Alien life?

During 1989 and 1990, thousands of people in Belgium witnessed bright, shining lights in the sky. They appeared night after night for six months. These UFOs seemed to be strange triangular objects. The Belgian government sent fighter jets to chase them, but the mysterious spacecraft were too fast to catch.

Air encounters

When people started flying aircraft, there were more and more reports of UFOs. **Second World War** fighter pilots told tales of mysterious aircraft that flashed by or followed them, before disappearing. They called them 'foo fighters'. Sometimes, people on the ground saw them, too. **Radar** readings have also shown strange aircraft in the skies that can't be explained.

The pilots of Second World War fighter planes spotted mysterious lights in the sky.

Alien life?

In 1947, Kenneth Arnold was shocked to see nine bright, flashing objects whizz past his light aircraft, near Mount Rainier, Washington, USA. He said they looked like saucers skipping across water. Since that day, many UFOs have been called flying saucers.

Could strange lights in the sky be
a spaceship from another planet?

Strange sighting

*In 1948, two boys were playing outside
in Minnesota, USA, when a grey disc landed
close to them. It was 70 centimetres across
and nearly 30 centimetres thick. It suddenly
spun into the sky and flew off. Later, an **FBI**
investigator found a flattened patch of ground
the same size as the disc the boys had described.*

Close encounters

Some people say they have met aliens who landed on Earth. They claim to have talked to them, too. Others say they have climbed on board an alien spacecraft. Can you imagine having such a close encounter?

There are many stories of alien encounters – could they be true?

Alien contact

Scientists say there are four types of encounter with an alien or a UFO.

1. Seeing an alien spaceship.
2. Finding **evidence** of an alien spaceship, such as heat marks on the ground.
3. Meeting an alien.
4. Being taken away by aliens for a short time.

Space creature

In 1952, George Adamski and his friends were having a picnic in the Mojave Desert in California, USA, when they saw a UFO in the sky. A **military** aircraft was chasing it. The UFO dropped a silver disc on the desert and George drove towards it. He said he met an alien creature, which claimed to be from the planet Venus.

George Adamski said he had other encounters with aliens, and was taken to the Moon in their spaceship.

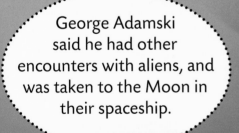

Men in black

Sometimes, people who have seen aliens have been visited afterwards by a small group of mysterious men wearing black clothes and dark glasses. The men have taken away any evidence of the sightings, such as photographs or videos.

Who are the 'men in black' who take away evidence of alien encounters?

The men have also told witnesses not to talk about the aliens they have seen. Some people think these men work for the government, while others believe they are aliens themselves.

Mysterious visit

In 1965, Rex Heflin took some photos of a UFO from his van in California, USA. Later, two men wearing black clothes visited him and demanded the photos. They said they were from the North American Aerospace Defense Command (NORAD), but the organization said that they had no record of them. No one knows who they were.

In 1952, prime minister Winston Churchill ordered a report into UFOs — but no one knows what it said.

Alien types

Do you know what an alien looks like?
People who have seen them usually describe
three types – greys, green men and reptilians.
Have a look around. Perhaps you've seen one?

Grey and green

The most common sightings are of greys. These aliens are shorter than humans. They have a big, bald head, large bulging dark eyes, a thin body and pale or grey skin. Most aliens have pale skin, but in 1947 Italian artist Rapuzzi Johannis was out walking when he saw two green aliens. These short creatures had large heads and hands with eight fingers.

Sometimes, aliens are called 'little green men'.

Reptilians

*Some people have seen aliens that look like **reptiles**. In 1967, Herbert Schirmer, a police officer from Nebraska, USA, said he had met a group of aliens who were about 1.5 metres tall, with long, thin heads. They had pale grey scaly skin, a flat nose, slanted eyes and a slit-like mouth. He said they wore tight silver suits, gloves and boots.*

Alien life?

In 1954, Jessie Roestenberg was shocked to see a large silver-coloured disc hovering above her house in Staffordshire. In fright, she hid under the kitchen table with her children. She said she saw two aliens in the spaceship. They had white skin, large foreheads and pale hair down to their shoulders.

Kidnap!

Imagine being kidnapped by an alien. Some people think aliens want to experiment on us. Others believe they want to warn us of future disasters.

Distant memory

Sometimes, people who claim to have been **abducted** by aliens can't describe where they were taken. Often their memories return a few weeks later. Some people find injuries on their bodies. Others have scary dreams.

Alien life?

In 1961, Betty and Barney Hill were driving in New Hampshire, USA, when they claim aliens kidnapped them. Barney saw a spacecraft flying towards them, then he and his wife passed out. Two hours later, they found themselves driving again. Later, they both had strange dreams. When a doctor **hypnotized** them, they both told similar stories.

People who claim to have been kidnapped by aliens often show signs of burns or small puncture wounds.

Canoe encounter

In 1976, four men were canoeing near Allagash, in Maine, USA, when a brightly-lit spacecraft flew over them. The men say they were taken from their boat for several hours. They couldn't remember what happened, but 12 years later, they all started to dream about bug-eyed creatures examining their bodies.

What happened to the men near Allagash when aliens abducted them?

Crash landings

Alien spacecraft probably crash from time to time. Some people believe that crashed UFOs are secretly hidden around the world.

Top secret!

Many people think that a UFO crashed near Roswell, New Mexico, USA, in 1947. They say the spaceship and its crew are kept in a secret location called Area 51, used for top-secret research. It is so secret that it does not appear on a map.

This model shows what an alien from Roswell might have looked like.

True or false?

Nearly 30 years later, people who had worked at the site claimed there had been a cover-up. They say the crash was kept secret. Some saw aliens in the aircraft. Others described an alien being interviewed and alien bodies being examined. No one really knows what happened.

Alien life?

In 1969, a UFO may have crashed in a remote part of Russia. A stolen film shows Russian soldiers examining an aircraft, which looks like a flying saucer partly buried in the ground. The Russian government says the incident did not take place. What do you think?

Still searching

The US space agency **NASA** hopes to answer some of the mysteries of the Universe one day. It has tried to contact aliens by beaming messages into space and sending spacecraft on unending journeys.

Space talk

Scientists think aliens may be trying to contact us, too. NASA is investigating all the **radio waves** coming to Earth from space, to see if there are any patterns which might be alien communication. However, no one speaks alien languages, so it's hard to know what to look for!

Radio telescopes detect signals from outer space.

Might the *Voyager* spacecraft make contact with alien life?

The golden records

In 1977, two NASA *Voyager spacecraft* travelled into outer space. Each had a gold disc on board with recordings of sounds from Earth, including a message in 55 languages. The discs also have pictures showing people and the position of Earth in space. Perhaps one day, aliens will find them!

Glossary

abducted
Taken away; kidnapped.

evidence
Facts or information used to prove something is true.

FBI
Federal Bureau of Investigation; a US police agency
investigating crimes or threats to national security.

hypnotized
When someone is hypnotized they go into a trance-like
state, in which they can hear and answer questions,
and may remember past events.

military
Belonging to the armed forces.

NASA
National Aeronautics and Space Administration;
a US agency responsible for aviation and spaceflight.

radar
A system that uses reflected radio waves to detect
aircraft, ships or other moving objects.

radio waves
> A type of radiation used for sending signals through the air.

reptiles
> Cold-blooded animals, such as snakes and lizards.

Second World War
A war fought from 1939 to 1945, in which the Allies (including the USA, Great Britain, France, the Soviet Union and China) defeated Germany, Italy and Japan.

Universe
Everything in space, including stars, planets and galaxies.

witnessed
Saw an event happen.

Websites

http://pbskids.org/arthur/games/alien/alien.html
What does an alien look like? Now you can draw your own!

http://www.kidzworld.com/article/1002-roswell-ufo-crash-site
Read more about UFO sightings at Roswell

Index